B AND BOY

Chad Norman

Cyberwit.net
HIG 45 Kaushambi Kunj, Kalindipuram
Allahabad - 211011 (U.P.) India
http://www.cyberwit.net
Tel: +(91) 9415091004
E-mail: info@cyberwit.net

Printed at Quarterfold Press.

*For all the children of Ukraine who have been
forced to begin new lives in new countries.*

ACKNOWLEDGEMENTS

First thing to say about this story is that it has not appeared in any publication anywhere. It has only been read aloud at the 2021 Honey Harvest festival, which takes place annually at the Avon River Heritage Museum, Newport Landing, Nova Scotia.

So, I just wish to say thanks to Tacha Reed, ten thousand thanks, in fact. Your illustrations continue to bring this story up off the page, and continue to leave me with tears of joy and gratitude.

As always, my Lainee and my Mikey, deserve a huge and loud thanks too. The love and support you continue to provide keeps me able to believe in the imagination.

And, lastly, another giant round of applause to Karunesh, all of those at Cyberwit, who worked on this book. My hats are all off!

FOREWORD

Sometimes the reader, meaning you, or a parent, or a person who loves to read stories, needs to know a little bit about the story before it is read. So, I wish to tell you, Boy, one of the characters in this story has lived in a number of Nova Scotia communities like Glenholme, Debert, Masstown, and Truro.

He hasn't always found it easy to have moved around, but I can say he is happy now that his Mum and Dad have found a home where his best friend B also lives, another character you will soon get to know.

Chad Norman
December 17, 2019

To have a name. Do you know your name? Who gave it to you? Mum? Dad?

Sometimes in some families it can be Gram or Gramp, they will choose to use nicknames like B and Boy.

And nicknames are only little names, shorter names, names given by others who have you in their hearts.

So for B and Boy names are kind of shortened or maybe kind of funny, like B for Bee, or Boy for Dave, Blake, or maybe even Chad.

To know your name. Do you have a nickname?
Who gave it to you? Bet you don't need one.

But two do B in the garden. Boy sitting
by a flower. Two starting this story!

A story about names and being safe. A story about
families. How the seasons change them, how B for-
gets about the cold.

And Boy visits the last of flowers, the few B seeks,
loading up on pollen the hive hopes to have be-
fore Winter.

And Boy watches B float from bloom to bloom,
legs loaded with the gold, watching as the wind
grows old.

B begins to stall, sitting still.

No buzz, saying nothing, the cold begins, and Boy watches some more, planning a kind of rescue.

B shivers in the Cosmos, sitting in the centre of the petals, and Boy knows that cold.

And Boy forgets his name, his name doesn't matter, he must save B, before the Winter longs to freeze.

Boy is quick to find a plan, simply what will help him understand B and other bees are wishing to keep warm.

Boy drips some honey in a bowl, one drop, two drops, big drops, ready to tell his mum, "I can save the bees!"

As for B the cold is no fun, to gather from the last of flowers, loading up his legs is hard work, but the hive needs his harvest.

So there is a day when it ends, Boy holds B in his fingers, places him in the honey, tries to begin to warm B.

There are others so cold, shivering in the flowers, pink and white Cosmos, too cold to go on.

Boy slowly picks them up too, places them beside B in the drops of honey, then takes them all inside.

A night in a house is all about getting warmed up, finding the honey to eat, sleeping together in one bed.

B snuggles with his cousins remembering the way to the hive, his cousins given the directions as the honey leaves their legs.

A morning is special when Boy takes them back to the tired garden the autumn sun has found, and places them in the last of the opened blooms, each one dancing in the last of the pollen, and B thanks Boy for a chance to sleep over, a chance to allow him and his cousins to live.

But B, even though a load weighs him down,
knows Boy is without, is without a pen, his way of
helping the world, having no hive, just those white
pages waiting somewhere to be filled.

Boy wanting to see the pen finally write his name,
write in c-u-r-s-i-v-e, Cursive!, kind of a big word
some of the adults say isn't important anymore.

Boy longing for someone to spell out who he is.

As the gate to the garden opens with a sound Boy
is surprised to see his grinning Gramp, one huge
hand holding a pen and the other reaching up to
the shirt pocket where he always kept a notebook.

Gramp sat down on the bucket not yet put away
for winter, his gentle voice then said,

"Come here, Boy, it is time, you are big enough
now to hold this pen, have me show you how to
write to spell out who you are, and to know your
name."

As they stood up the notebook fell out of the coat worn on Sundays, Gramp's smile got bigger when Boy picked it up and tried to give it back, Boy looked up at him when he said,

 "No, you keep it, the pen too. Use them both to learn how to *write* your name. I know you can print it. Go ahead, give it a try!"

A cold wind came up again, Gramp closed the gate, Boy stopped to look, to try and see if B and those happy cousins were gone from the garden.

Boy smiled this time, he knew they made it, to the hive, their home.

Gramp waved from his truck. The day began to darken, Boy saw the lights in the home where he lives, he put the pen in his shirt pocket, and poked at the notebook as the front-door quietly closed.

Boy went down the stairs to sit on his big comfy bed, he opened the notebook and looked at the lines, putting the pen down on one he thought of Gramp's words, "...give it a try!".

So he did, making what he saw as a mark, his mark, trying to write, write the letters, trying to write what would always be his name, what began to fill each and every empty page.

Mum Mum
DAD Dad
Gram Gram
Gramp Gramp
Chad Chad
Chad Chad
Chad Chad
Chad Ch
B B B B
B B
B B B
B B C C
B C C

Tomorrow was a school day, Boy thought about his desk, about the big black-board, how his teacher may ask him to pick up a piece of chalk, and do what his pen is doing.

Boy thought about how he will look up and see the letters, A-B-C-D, all of them pinned to the wall, with their curls and swirls, up there for all to finally see.

Boy had one more thought, he will write his name, and beside it one more, to remember a new friend, and watch as his hand also writes, B is for bee, b-e-e!

Kk Ll Mm Nn Oo
B is for bee

AFTERWORD

Sometimes, at the end of a story, something else needs to be told. I don't know if you noticed but B has certain flowers and gardens to visit, the ones liked best, so you should know where they are. But first of all I need to tell you that B comes from out the Millbrook and Stewiacke way. Yes! I know, that can be where you didn't think of, but not only does B fly that far, many bees now have to fly away from their hives to find what will become the honey you say you really like. B wants to keep on finding those flowers, so maybe you can plant some in your yard. And, finally, it you don't know yet how to write your name, learn and practice it. If you already do know how look up and smile. Always remember, Boy does now too!

Thank you for reading my story.

Chad Norman

December 2019